HOW TO DRAW ACTION FIGHTING FIGURES ™

Mark Bergin

BOOK HOUSE

S A L A R I Y A

Published in Great Britain in MMXII by
Book House, an imprint of
The Salariya Book Company Ltd
25 Marlborough Place, Brighton BN1 1UB

1 3 5 7 9 8 6 4 2

Please visit our website at **www.salariya.com**
for **free** electronic versions of:
You Wouldn't Want to Be an Egyptian Mummy!
You Wouldn't Want to Be a Roman Gladiator!
You Wouldn't Want to be a Polar Explorer!
You Wouldn't want to Sail on a 19th-Century
Whaling Ship!

Author: Mark Bergin was born in Hastings in 1961.
He studied at Eastbourne College of Art and has
specialised in historical reconstructions as well as
aviation and maritime subjects since 1983. He lives
in Bexhill-on-Sea with his wife and three children.

Editor: Rob Walker

PB ISBN: 978-1-908177-19-3

A CIP catalogue record for this
book is available from the
British Library.

Printed and bound in China.
Printed on paper from
sustainable sources.

**WARNING: Fixatives should be
used only under adult supervision.**

PAPER FROM
SUSTAINABLE
FORESTS

Contents

Making a start

Learning to draw is about looking and seeing. Keep practising and get to know your subject. Use a sketchbook to make quick drawings. Start by doodling, and experiment with shapes and patterns. There are many ways to draw; this book shows only some methods. Visit art galleries, look at artists' drawings, see how friends draw, but above all, find your own way.

Drawing materials

Try using different types of drawing paper and materials. Experiment with charcoal, wax crayons and pastels. All pens, from felt—tips to ballpoints, will make interesting marks — you could also try drawing with pen and ink on wet paper.

Silhouette

Silhouette is a style of drawing which mainly uses solid black shapes.

Felt—tip

Felt—tips come in a range of line widths. The wider pens are good for filling in large areas of flat tone.

6

Hard **pencils** are greyer and soft pencils are blacker. Hard pencils are graded from 6H (the hardest) through 5H, 4H, 3H and 2H to H. Soft pencils are graded from B, 2B, 3B, 4B and 5B up to 6B (the softest).

Pencil

Lines drawn in **ink** cannot be erased, so keep your ink drawings sketchy and less rigid. Don't worry about mistakes as these lines can be lost in the drawing as it develops.

Ink

7

Perspective

If you look at any object from different viewpoints, you will see that the part that is closest to you looks larger, and the part furthest away from you looks smaller. Drawing in perspective is a way of creating a feeling of depth – of showing three dimensions on a flat surface.

V.P.

The vanishing point (V.P.) is the place in a perspective drawing where parallel lines appear to meet. The position of the vanishing point depends on the viewer's eye level. Sometimes a low viewpoint can give your drawing added drama.

V.P.

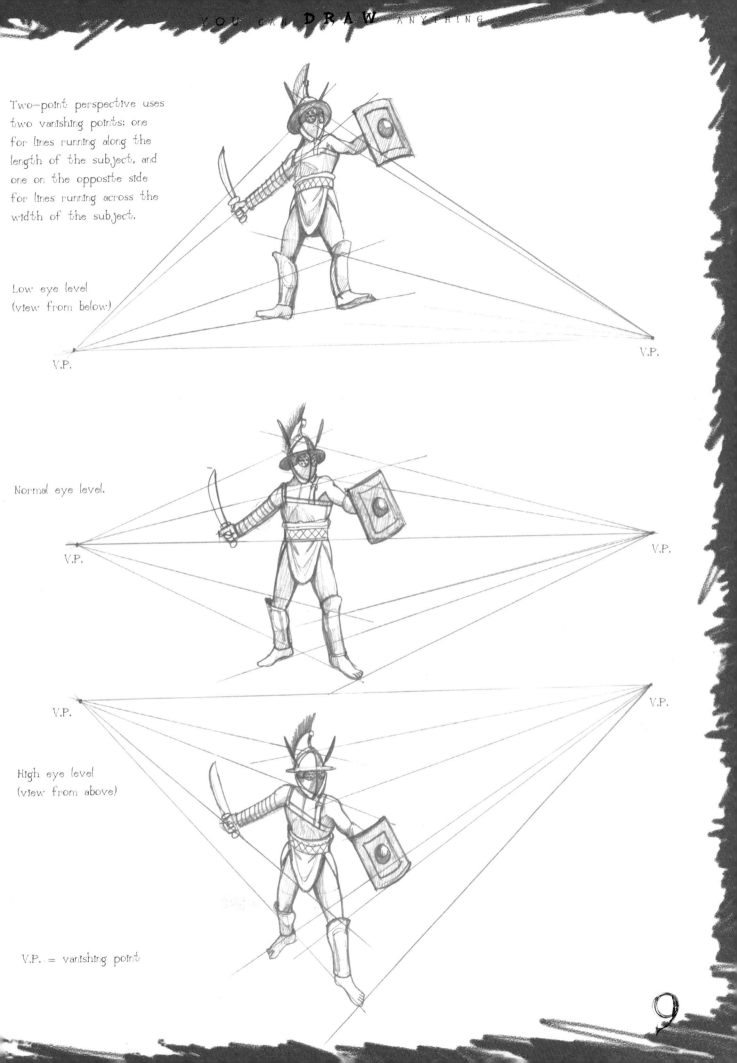

Two-point perspective uses two vanishing points: one for lines running along the length of the subject, and one on the opposite side for lines running across the width of the subject.

Low eye level (view from below)

V.P.

V.P.

Normal eye level.

V.P.

V.P.

V.P.

High eye level (view from above)

V.P. = vanishing point

Using photos

Drawing from photographs of real fighting figures can help you develop your drawing skills and also your eye for detail.

Make a tracing of a photograph and draw a grid of squares over it.

Now draw another grid on your drawing paper, enlarging or reducing the squares but keeping the same proportions as your tracing grid. You can now copy the shapes from each square of your tracing to your drawing paper, using the grid as a guide.

To make your drawing look three-dimensional, decide which side the light is coming from, and put in areas of shadow on the opposite side.

Sketch in an overall tone to create interest and a sense of movement. Pay attention to the position of the figures on the paper; this is called composition.

11

Action poses

Practise basic poses and quick stick figure drawings to get a sense of action into your basic poses. Getting the movement right in these early stages will make your completed drawing look better.

Boxing

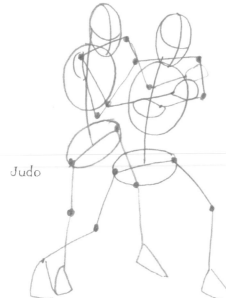

Judo

Swordfight

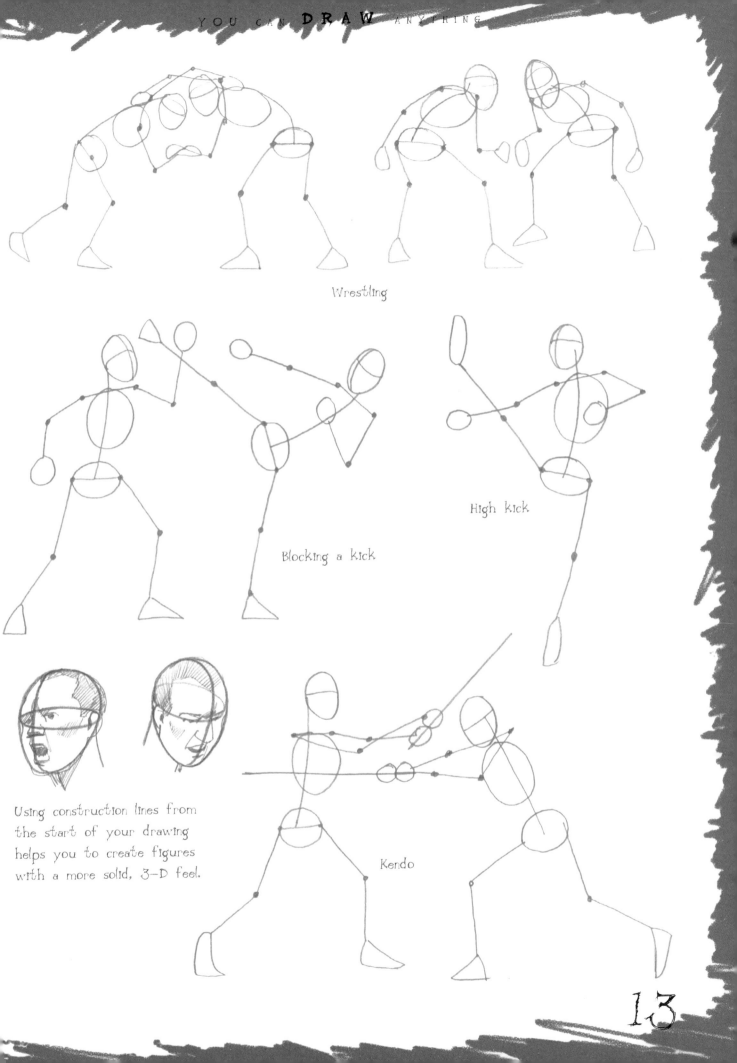

Wrestling

Blocking a kick

High kick

Using construction lines from the start of your drawing helps you to create figures with a more solid, 3-D feel.

Kendo

13

Ninja assassin

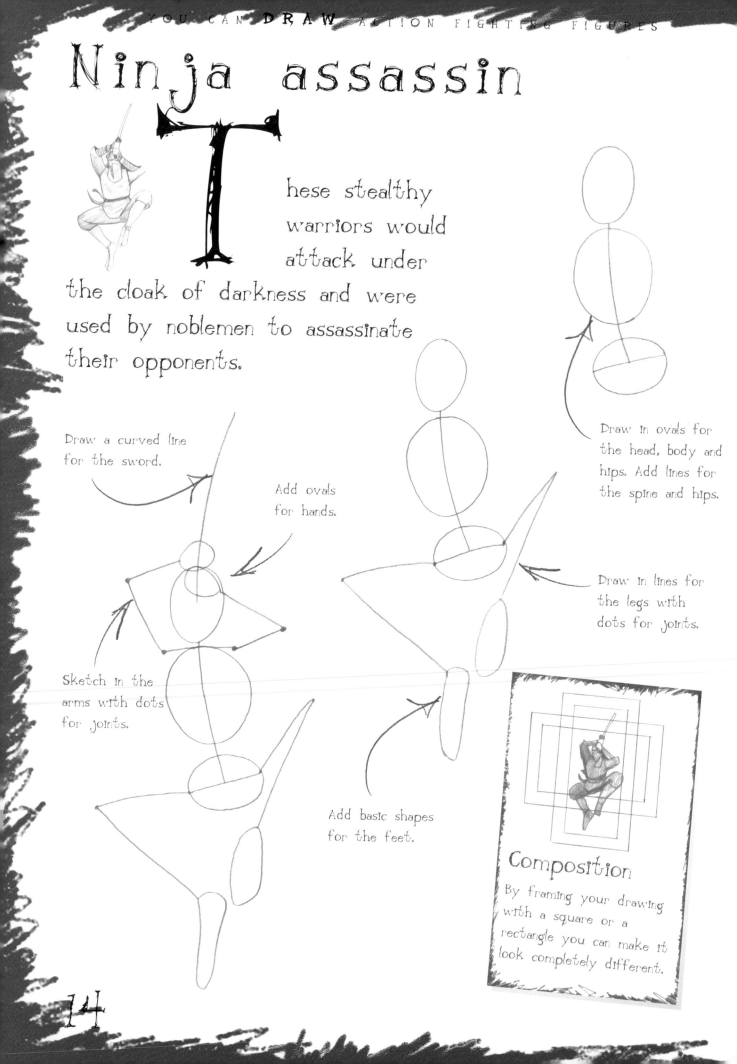

T hese stealthy warriors would attack under the cloak of darkness and were used by noblemen to assassinate their opponents.

Draw a curved line for the sword.

Add ovals for hands.

Draw in ovals for the head, body and hips. Add lines for the spine and hips.

Draw in lines for the legs with dots for joints.

Sketch in the arms with dots for joints.

Add basic shapes for the feet.

Composition

By framing your drawing with a square or a rectangle you can make it look completely different.

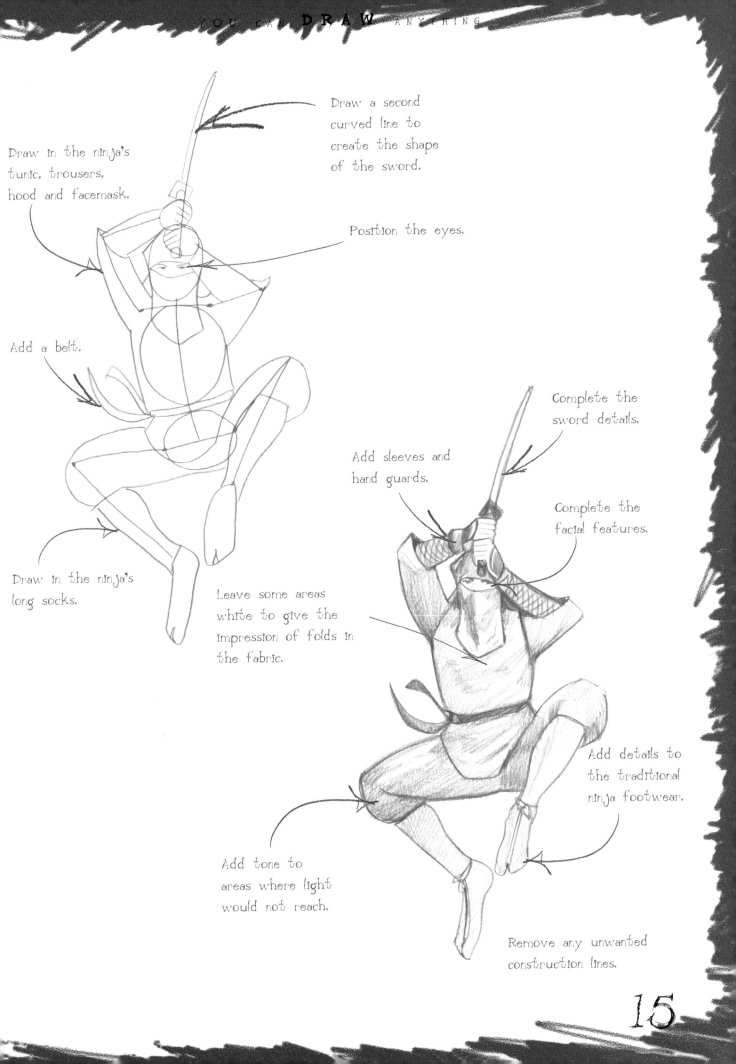

Draw in the ninja's tunic, trousers, hood and facemask.

Draw a second curved line to create the shape of the sword.

Position the eyes.

Add a belt.

Complete the sword details.

Add sleeves and hand guards.

Complete the facial features.

Draw in the ninja's long socks.

Leave some areas white to give the impression of folds in the fabric.

Add details to the traditional ninja footwear.

Add tone to areas where light would not reach.

Remove any unwanted construction lines.

15

Karate

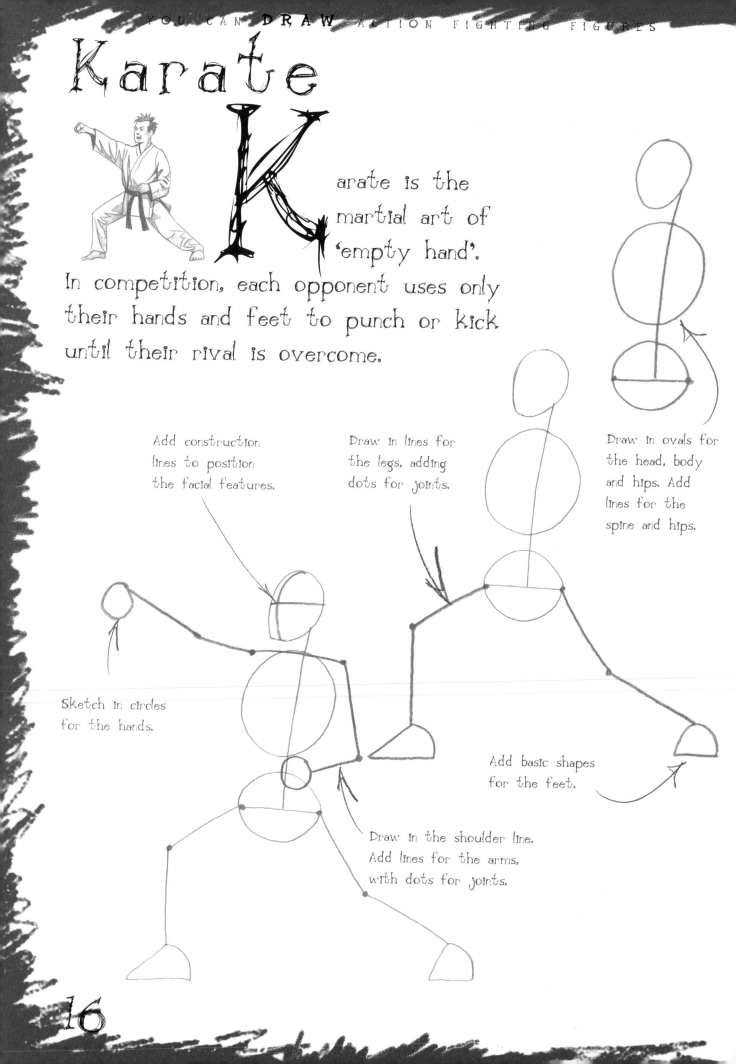

Karate is the martial art of 'empty hand'. In competition, each opponent uses only their hands and feet to punch or kick until their rival is overcome.

Draw in ovals for the head, body and hips. Add lines for the spine and hips.

Add construction lines to position the facial features.

Draw in lines for the legs, adding dots for joints.

Sketch in circles for the hands.

Add basic shapes for the feet.

Draw in the shoulder line. Add lines for the arms, with dots for joints.

Add spiky hair.

Sketch in the expressive facial features using the construction lines as a guide.

Draw in the shape of the clenched fist inside the circle.

Add the tunic of the karategi (the karate uniform).

Draw in a belt.

Add the karategi trousers.

Add more detail to the shape of the feet.

Finish drawing the fist.

Complete the facial details.

Add tone to areas where light wouldn't reach.

Add lines and tone to show the folds in the karategi.

Add tone to the belt.

Finish off the feet.

Remove any unwanted construction lines.

17

Karate kick

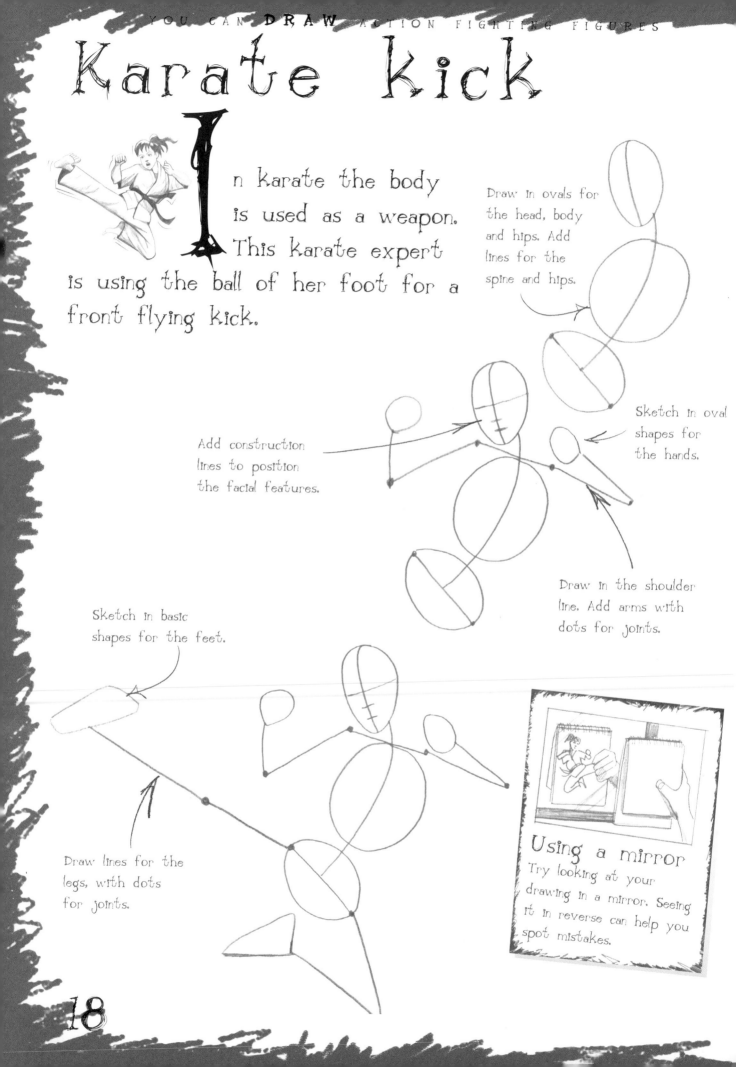

In karate the body is used as a weapon. This karate expert is using the ball of her foot for a front flying kick.

Draw in ovals for the head, body and hips. Add lines for the spine and hips.

Add construction lines to position the facial features.

Sketch in oval shapes for the hands.

Draw in the shoulder line. Add arms with dots for joints.

Sketch in basic shapes for the feet.

Draw lines for the legs, with dots for joints.

Using a mirror
Try looking at your drawing in a mirror. Seeing it in reverse can help you spot mistakes.

Draw in facial features using the construction lines.

Draw the hair. The direction will emphasise movement.

Add toes and shape to the feet.

Add detail to the fists and forearms.

Position the belt.

Draw in the karategi trousers and tunic.

Add tone to the hair.

Complete all details of the feet.

Add tone and detail to the fists and forearms.

Finish off facial details.

Complete the belt and add dark tone.

Add dark tone to areas light wouldn't reach.

Add tone to show folds in the karategi.

Remove any unwanted construction lines.

Add movement lines.

19

Samurai battle

Samurai warriors fought in accordance with Japanese rules of honour and pride. They used a range of weapons which included incredibly sharp swords called katanas.

Draw in ovals for the heads, bodies and hips. Add lines for the spines and hips.

This samurai is seen in profile so the line of the spine is on the left hand side.

Sketch in ovals for the hands.

Add lines for the arms, with dots for the joints.

Add lines for the blade of each sword.

Add lines for the legs, with dots for the joints.

Draw in basic shapes for the feet.

Add hair to each samurai.

Draw in the facial features.

Sketch in more shape to each sword.

Each samurai's robe is tied at the centre.

Using the construction lines as a guide, add the samurai's traditional clothing.

Add tone to areas where light wouldn't reach.

Finish off the facial details.

Add tone to the hair.

Add lines and tone to show folds in the fabric. Leave some areas white.

Complete the detail of the clothing by adding a pattern.

Finish the details of the feet.

Complete the details of each costume.

Remove any unwanted construction lines.

Armoured samurai

These two heavily armoured samurai are from the Genpei War. The striking katana (samurai sword) is being blocked by the naginata (the staff).

Draw in ovals for the heads, bodies and hips. Add lines for the spines and hips.

Add lines for the arms, with dots for the joints.

Add a long line with a curved end for the naginata.

Draw in basic shapes for the helmets.

Add basic hand shapes.

Draw in basic shapes for the feet.

Draw in lines for the legs, with dots for the joints.

Complete the shape of the naginata.

Draw in fingers on each hand.

Add the complex decoration of the helmets.

Draw in the sleeves and wide samurai trousers.

Draw in the facial features.

Add the large plates of armour.

Sketch in the legs, indicating armour.

Add tone to areas light wouldn't reach.

Complete the samurai helmets and costume detail.

Add zig-zag details to the armour to show how it is made.

Finish the facial features.

Add tone to show shape and movement of trousers.

Complete the details of the naginata and katana.

Add armour to the legs and complete the feet.

Remove any unwanted construction lines.

23

Kendo

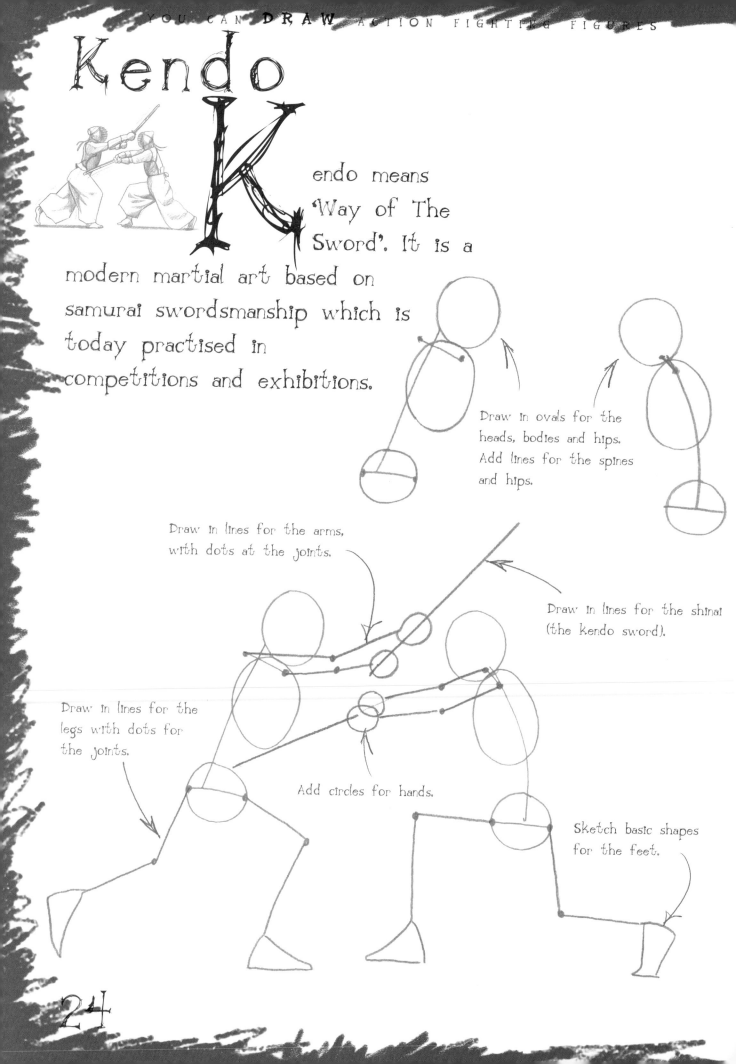

Kendo means 'Way of The Sword'. It is a modern martial art based on samurai swordsmanship which is today practised in competitions and exhibitions.

Draw in ovals for the heads, bodies and hips. Add lines for the spines and hips.

Draw in lines for the arms, with dots at the joints.

Draw in lines for the shinai (the kendo sword).

Draw in lines for the legs with dots for the joints.

Add circles for hands.

Sketch basic shapes for the feet.

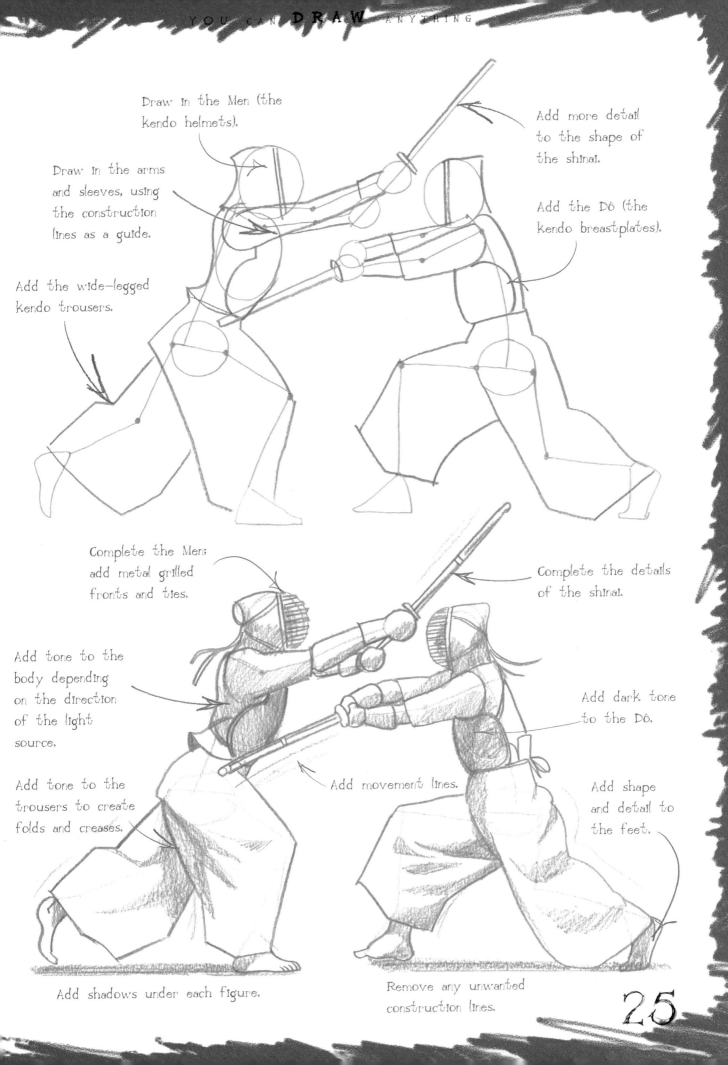

Draw in the Men (the kendo helmets).

Draw in the arms and sleeves, using the construction lines as a guide.

Add the wide-legged kendo trousers.

Add more detail to the shape of the shinai.

Add the Dō (the kendo breastplates).

Complete the Men; add metal grilled fronts and ties.

Complete the details of the shinai.

Add tone to the body depending on the direction of the light source.

Add dark tone to the Dō.

Add tone to the trousers to create folds and creases.

Add movement lines.

Add shape and detail to the feet.

Add shadows under each figure.

Remove any unwanted construction lines.

25

Greek warriors

These two Bronze age Greek hoplite warriors are from warring states. They are fighting shield to shield. Cities like Athens and Sparta were deadly enemies, fighting for supremacy over land and trade routes.

Draw in ovals for the heads, bodies and hips. Add lines for the spines and hips.

Draw two large ovals for shields.

Draw in a line for each sword.

Draw in lines for the arms, with dots for the joints.

Add circles for the hands.

Sketch in lines for the legs, with dots for the joints.

Sketch in basic shapes for the feet.

Add more detail to the swords.

Draw in the distinctive helmet shapes.

Draw in the shape of the arms, using the construction lines as a guide.

Add the curved decoration to each helmet.

Sketch in the body armour and tunics.

Add shape to the legs, using the construction lines as a guide.

Draw in the leg armour.

Add designs and battle scars to each shield.

Complete all details to each helmet.

Add tone to the arms.

Add hair.

Complete all details of the armour.

Add both scabbards.

Add tone to the leg armour.

Add toes and all details of the feet.

Add tone to areas light wouldn't reach.

Remove any unwanted construction lines.

Judo

Judo is a modern martial art. Its name means the 'gentle way'. The object of a competition is to throw an opponent to the ground, immobilising them, and to force their submission using specific manoeuvres.

Draw in ovals for the heads, bodies and hips. Add lines for the spines and hips.

Draw in lines for the arms, with dots for the joints. The arms overlap as the figures grab hold of each other.

Add basic shapes for hands.

Sketch in construction lines to position the facial features.

Add lines for the legs, with dots for the joints.

Draw in basic shapes for the feet.

Using the construction lines as a guide, add the tunic of the judogi (the judo uniform).

Draw in the hairline.

Add the belts.

Sketch in the basic details of each face.

Use the construction line to draw in the judogi trousers.

Pay careful attention to which leg is in front of which.

Add detail to the hands.

Finish off the hair and facial features.

Add dark tone to the belts.

Add tone to areas where light wouldn't reach.

Add lines and tone to show folds and movement in the fabric.

Add toes and complete the feet.

Remove any unwanted construction lines.

29

Roman gladiators

The roman gladiatorial games were loved by all in ancient Rome.

Here a Retiarius (with a net and trident) battles a Myrmillo, a 'heavy armed' gladiator with a sword and shield.

Draw in ovals for the heads, bodies and hips. Add lines for the spines and hips.

Add a helmet to the Myrmillo.

Draw in a shield.

Draw in lines for the arms, with dots for the joints.

Draw in ovals and circles for hands.

Add a long line for the shaft of the trident.

Draw a line to position the sword.

Add lines for the legs with dots for the joints.

Draw in basic shapes for the feet.

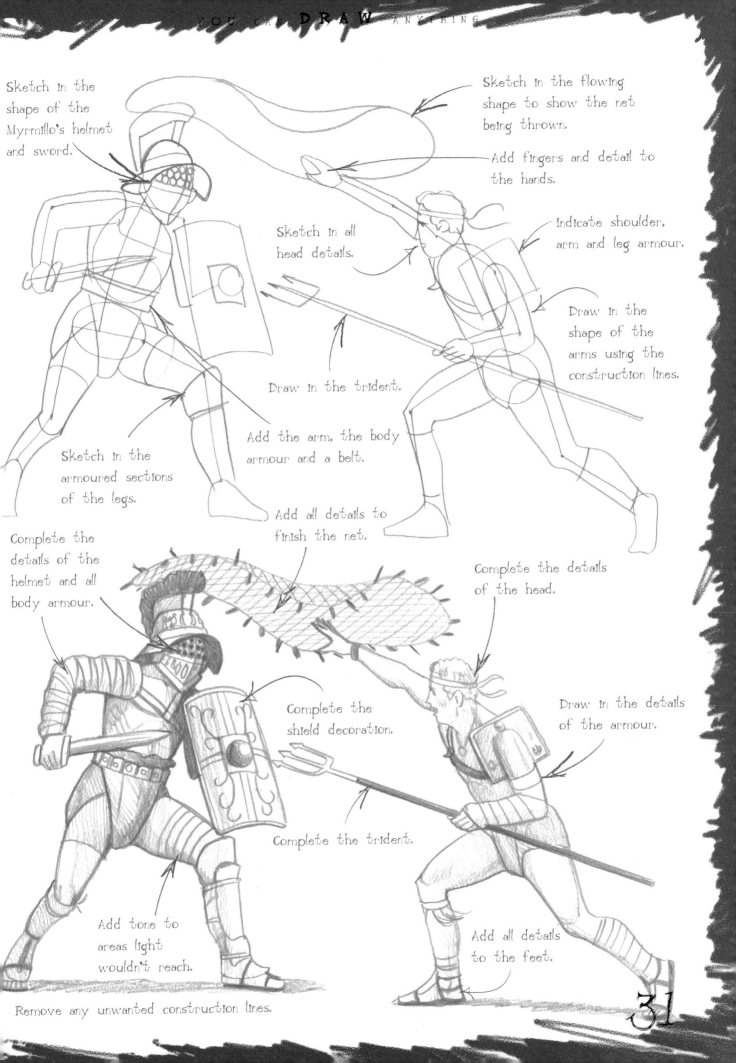

Sketch in the shape of the Myrmillo's helmet and sword.

Sketch in the flowing shape to show the net being thrown.

Add fingers and detail to the hands.

Sketch in all head details.

Indicate shoulder, arm and leg armour.

Draw in the shape of the arms using the construction lines.

Draw in the trident.

Add the arm, the body armour and a belt.

Sketch in the armoured sections of the legs.

Add all details to finish the net.

Complete the details of the helmet and all body armour.

Complete the details of the head.

Complete the shield decoration.

Draw in the details of the armour.

Complete the trident.

Add tone to areas light wouldn't reach.

Add all details to the feet.

Remove any unwanted construction lines.

31

Glossary

Composition The arrangement of the parts of a picture on the drawing paper.

Construction lines Guidelines used in the early stages of a drawing. They are usually erased later.

Fixative A type of resin used to spray over a finished drawing to prevent smudging. **It should only be used by an adult.**

Light source The direction from which the light seems to come in a drawing.

Perspective A method of drawing in which near objects are shown larger than faraway objects to give an impression of depth.

Pose The position assumed by a figure.

Proportion The correct relationship of scale between each part of the drawing.

Silhouette A drawing that shows only a flat, dark shape, like a shadow.

Vanishing point The place in a perspective drawing where parallel lines appear to meet.

Index